Give Me a Year

An Essay for Leaders and Teachers That
Labor in Redemptive Love and Sacrifice

DONETRUS G. HILL, EdD

WESTBOW
PRESS®
A DIVISION OF THOMAS NELSON
& ZONDERVAN

WestBow Press books may be ordered through booksellers or by contacting:

WestBow Press
A Division of Thomas Nelson & Zondervan
1663 Liberty Drive
Bloomington, IN 47403
www.westbowpress.com
1 (866) 928-1240

Scripture taken from the King James Version of the Bible.

ISBN: 978-1-9736-5336-3 (sc)
ISBN: 978-1-9736-5338-7 (hc)
ISBN: 978-1-9736-5337-0 (e)

Library of Congress Control Number: 2019901660

Print information available on the last page.

WestBow Press rev. date: 5/15/2019

I dedicate this book and all future publications to the memory of sportscaster, journalist, son, and my younger brother, Rondray Latrell Hill.

August 1, 1980–May 25, 2002

Your life will continue to evolve with each volume this family commits to print!

Signature Page

Let me be the first to say, "Happy New Year!"

Give Me a Year lives boldly in you!

My Greatest Inspiration

To Cornelia and Roman. The both of you have selflessly given up so much for me to complete this volume. I now give this testament back to the both of you.

The two of you are my greatest inspiration.

Let's have an amazing year for the rest of our lives!

Contents

Foreword

God speaks to us in divers manners and in many instances. While we are experiencing a moment of despondency, perhaps that's the time our sensitivity to the Spirit is keenest, and God can download into us His perfect plan for our lives.

Dr. Hill shares his heart about God's leading, as well as His plan and purpose for his life. Oftentimes God causes us to remember a scripture and reflect on the moment of the test, and that causes us to rejoice and celebrate its revelation for our lives, opening a vast new season for our lives.

A year is divided into four seasons, and each season has its implications in our lives. Many of us need to experience the four seasons of life to recover from the failures, defeats, and bitterness of our past. I call this the "miracle of the second chance." *Give Me a Year* will bless your life. Read it and meditate on it. Allow the Holy Spirit to reveal your potential, abilities, giftings, and anointings that are lying dormant in your life. Take another year to break up the fallow ground, sow good seeds, and germinate into a new life.

> And he shall be like a tree planted by the rivers of water, and bring forth his fruit in his season, his leaf also shall not wither, and whatever he doeth shall prosper. (Psalm 1:3)

Give me another year—my season of productivity and truth in the year.

It is my desire that this book will stir you to move forward into your new year of destiny.

Bishop Truman L. Martin, DDS
October 2018

Introduction: Give Me a Year

It was a cold February afternoon in Dayton Ohio—Super Bowl Sunday, to be exact. I placed an announcement on Facebook letting my followers know I was going live at 2:00 p.m. EST. I was building my audience. I had enough sense to know when you have something to say, you need people to listen—just as when you are a leader, there must be a collection of followers. If you look behind and see no one is there, whom or what are you leading? But it's too early to get into that type of thinking. Let me continue to set the stage for *Give Me a Year*.

Before I get too far ahead of myself, I deem it necessary to take you back to January 7, 2018, the first Sunday of the new year. It snowed all night, leaving a silky canvas of white on the trees and yards. Truly a majestic sight to see, but not to drive on. I got up that morning and debated with myself as to whether or not I was going to place my precious Cadillac on those icy, freshly salted roads or watch a sermon on the Internet. Unfortunately, there was no anointing on the Internet, and so I knew I had to get out in the elements. But the one thing about elements is if used correctly, they give and sustain life (that is the science teacher and biology major in me).

I trusted the elements and attended Maranatha Worship Center, where Bishop Truman Martin is the presiding prelate (and established dentist in the city). Bishop Martin was in rare form that morning. He delivered a fiery message, speaking about what God is prepared to do for those who believe and have enough faith to conceive. I was glad I'd made the right choice. I and the other congregants were inclined to listen further. When I attend worship services, I continue to read scripture while the minister delivers the message. I am a reader and like to see what the scripture says for myself. I encourage you to do the same. In all aspects of life, seek out information for yourself. Do not take everyone's word at face value. It's like Ronald Reagan said: "Trust, but verify."

Here is proof you must read for yourself. Finish this for me: "The race is not given to the swift, nor the battle to the strong, [finish it here]." I am certain many of you said, "to the one that endureth to the end." Now, if you have your Bible, turn with me to Ecclesiastes 9:11. What does it say? Again, trust, but verify. The true essence of learning takes place when the realization of truth or facts unknown become common to you based on your personalized study. When acquiring knowledge, seek out several sources before drawing an infinite conclusion.

Okay, back to the service! Bishop Martin preached the story of the fig tree that bore no fruit, found in Luke 13:6–9. In this parable, there was a man who owned a vineyard. On his vineyard, there was a fig tree that bore no fruit. The owner of the tree spoke to the gardener and stated that for three years, he had come to the tree to view its branches in anticipation of finding fruit, only to be disappointed because it had yet to bear any fruit. He insisted that the keeper of the vineyard cut the tree down. His argument was based on the premise that allowing the tree to consume the elements and nutrients found in the ground was a waste. He stated that something more productive and gratifying could be grown in its place. He was looking for a tree that would satisfy his appetite immediately. Isn't that just like us? We want what we want, when we want it. No time for excuses because excuses don't excuse, and explanations don't explain. If we don't see what we want to see when we want to see it, we are prepared to move on to something else. From this, please begin to emulate patience. You may be tired of a situation or job that is not productive. Instead of quitting, be patient. Good things come to those who wait. They may be getting on your nerves, but trust me; at some point they will get off them, and you will begin to appreciate your profession again. Patience is the key to overcoming. Oftentimes, quitting only provides temporary relief. Walking away from tasks incomplete or assignments unfulfilled may bring about a sensation of gratification and vindication, but how many of us have termed relationships, be it personal or professional, only to be miserable a few days later, sitting with a tumultuous amount of regret—and in some instances inconceivable debt? Give it time. As scripture records, "Be anxious for nothing."

This is also the case in education. Districts often get a new curriculum program, or a new principal is selected, or there is an update to testing expectations, or there's a new system of intervention in response to student-based trauma, or extreme learning gaps are introduced when you just got a handle on the last one the district invested in. Whatever the case may be, someone has made the decision to go in a new direction. Do you know how frustrating that is—and moreover, how often it occurs? In life, situations such as the ones listed above are not uncommon. They happen all the time.

To continue with the parable from the book of Luke, in a calm and reassuring voice, the gardener says to the owner of the vineyard, "Leave it alone. Let me till the ground, aerate it, fertilize it, and water it." In essence, what he was saying was, "I know how it looks. It looks like there is no hope for this tree [student], but I believe there is life still worth living for this tree. This tree has not seen its best days. There is so much untapped promise and potential here. I believe if we encourage the tree, love the tree, embrace the tree, find a healthy balance of nutrients for the tree, and allow the interventions to strengthen and encourage the tree, then we will see what we want from the tree in time!" Notice I did not say tomorrow or at the end of the season or semester, but rather in time.

The tree needed an advocate, which is the case for our students today. If we are honest, at some point in time in our lives, we have all needed or will need an advocate—someone who will stand up for us against status quo thinking. Someone who will place his or her credibility and reputation on the line for the belief that a situation or a person still has merit and value. That the situation is still worth the effort, worth the fight. That this is not the end but rather an opportunity to intervene and make someone else's life and reality a tad bit better. As leaders and believers, we have to champion the message that there is still life that can emerge from a place of darkness, depravity, stagnation, and inactivity. I declare to each of you that no matter what the scenario, declare in your mind that as a leader, a person of faith, and an advocate for the voiceless or disenfranchised,

"I am not going to give up on them or their situation! I too can make a difference!"

In the parable, the main character is a tree. However, each of us has had to respond to similar situations either personally or professionally, where we needed to take a stance on behalf of others. It could be a marriage on the brink of divorce, a relationship where maturity is not always present, a child who has turned to gangs because he is seeking love and attention, a father battling drug or alcohol abuse, or a female who has not realized her virtue and beauty and believes that her talents are below her waist and not above her shoulders. Maybe it's a position or promotion you know someone deserved, but politics was the deciding factor and not dedication, productivity, talent, and ability. We each have a responsibility to push back against bureaucracy and systems that devalue the process of hard work and equitable advancement. People are losing hope because of systems they can't interpret. Because they don't have a certain look or are not the envisioned color, weight, gender, or religion, they miss out on well-deserved opportunities. Again, we all need an advocate to push back against fixed thinking and both covert and overt gestures of intolerance, discrimination, and racism.

Irrespective of the scenario, there comes a time in each of our lives where we must make a decision that will impact either us or someone else. The reason for this is to afford them an opportunity to transition from an inactive state of being to making a concerted effort in determining the best course of action and manufacturing fruit that will sustain them and their families for many days to come. We can't give up on life because we are hungry and have yet to bear fruit. We have to take the lessons life provides, put our hands into the soil of our own lives, and unearth the dead places. It's not to discard them, but rather to refer to them as we make strides toward production. When was the last time you tasted the fruit you bear? Is it sweet or bitter? Is it plentiful? Do you need to do self-inventory and assess your own living to see where you can make adjustments in order to improve the fruit you bear? Is your fruit succulent and savory, or is it dry and bitter?

We all need to aerate our own soil, turn it over, and let some new oxygen into our orifice. Let a fresh wind bring new pollen to our situation so that we can bloom pretty flowers that speak to the beauty we now embrace because of the ashes we endured (Isaiah 61:3). God promised us beauty for ashes. What you need to know is ashes, if introduced into the soil early enough, support the growth of beautiful flowers. All the destruction, heartache, and pain you have endured on the job, in the classroom, at your home, with your children, or wherever you have experienced perceived destruction will bless you in time. Fret not, beloved; the ashes have been collected and introduced into the soil (soul) of your life. Its purpose is that it will be used to perfect your beauty and restore your value. Trust the process and let God use his elements to restore and refine you.

To finish the parable, the gardener stated to the owner, "After I do all this to the ground surrounding the tree, leave it alone for a year. Let us see if the interventions work. If the tree produces fruit, great. If not, do what you must and cut it down."

I know it took time to get to this point, but from that moment, after I read the part about give the tree one year to show its value and ability to produce fruit, God gave me the vision of *Give Me a Year*!

For exactly one month, everything I posted on Facebook included *Give Me a Year*. My peers began asking what it meant. I refused to answer their questions because I felt it was personal. But on February 4, 2018, God informed me that the message was not just for me but for the world. So at 2:00 p.m. on Super Bowl Sunday, I put on my New Orleans Saints jersey and introduced *Give Me a Year* to the world. (And yes, I know the Saints were not in the Super Bowl. However, I am not a bandwagoner!)

Give Me a Year Defined

Give Me a Year, in its most fundamental interpretation, is the plea for us to not give up on our lives, dreams, and goals.

To be bold and consistent in our quest to accomplish the most outlandish of aspirations. Do not succumb to societal norms. Live out loud and embrace the things about you that make you, you. Do not give up on your life, marriage, relationship, children, family, career, degree, ministry, weight-loss goals, writing a book, starting a business, or buying a house. You name it, and I am claiming that it is worth you giving it a full year in order to accomplish it and see if it can produce fruit once it comes into its season. Nothing is promised, and as long as what you are doing is not toxic, abusive, or corrosive, you owe it to yourself, you owe it to your family, and you owe it to God to let time and chance happen to you. Don't give up, though the pace seems slow. You have to commit your life, energy, and works toward accomplishing a goal. It is not going to be easy, but it is possible.

Give Me a Year also speaks to many failures and disappointments you've experienced. The impetus of the message is to affirm the fact that your life and your legacy are not destroyed. You can and will rebound from your past or even current state of misery or confusion. Your suffering will produce something amazing. You have not endured hardship this long for nothing, but rather for a purpose beyond what you can see. Remember to let patience be introduced into the equation of your life.

So what if you failed? Failing is a necessary part of life.

Who cares that it didn't work out? Being disappointed is a necessary part of life. But remember this: being disappointed is a part of life, but being discouraged is a choice. You have to choose to live life until you can experience life. Let me say that again, in case you read it too fast: you have to live life until you can truly experience life. Life is for the living! Life is happening to each of us at a considerable rate of speed. Time is flying. It is time for each of us to reclaim our time and live out loud! In order to do that, you have to make a choice to start enjoying life and being better in it. The way to do it is to embrace what comes and make the most out of every situation. Do not get frustrated and discouraged when outmatched or outwitted, but rather focus your time, energy, and effort in committing a year of studying, observing, or learning to ensure that when the opportunity presents itself next, you are more prepared. The beautiful thing about declaring your year is you can begin the year of liberation any day or time you decide. You can make the choice today to fight for the next year to enjoy the rest of your life. *Give Me a Year* is about living a life full of passion and purpose for all. It matters not your age, race, religion, or color. It is for all. It is the year that God gave you to work out your issues and challenges. Embrace it, possess it, aerate it, improve it, and then live it out loud!

To the educators who put it on the line each and every day, take the next year, embrace three strategies, and let them act as Novocain. Anesthetize the situations in your classroom, and once things have become less painful, get to work. Improve your relationships with parents and students. Improve your instructional practices to provide struggling students the best first taught instruction possible, which by design is our greatest intervention used to eradicate failure. Commit to professional growth, training, and development in order to mature and sophisticate your craft. And to the principals and central office personnel: listen to your staff more. Listen to your parents and students as well; they have insight you don't have. Trust those among whom you labor. Be more personable and approachable. Expose them to some of your vulnerabilities as well. Let them see that if cut, you bleed too. Take the next year and embrace those whom trust you to educate and lead them.

Give Me a Year is about this being the best year of your life to impact and carve out the rest of your life. It is more than a notion. It is a revolutionary, transformative way of thinking. This type of level four (Webb's Depth of Knowledge, or DOK) thinking is for bold individuals who are tired of business as usual. They are about reclaiming their time, thinking outside the box, and living lives driven by growth and development.

Give Me a Year is for the collection of believers who choose to be emancipated from a fixed, deficit mindset. They are tired of crawling—they are ready to soar! *Give Me a Year* is the beginning of a life worth living and a legacy worth leaving. No matter who or what you are, you can choose to cast down the chains of bondage from your life and set free a legion of captives. Many of you are the answer to someone's prayers. They are watching you to see how you handle life this year. Show them what hard work and dedication toward a life lived on purpose can produce. If you are ready to give yourself a year, then let's do this!

Give Me a Year!

Please take time and give considerable thought to the questions listed below. Answer with your honest, most intimate reflections in an effort to setup the most amazing year(s) of your life. Remember, you deserve it!

- List three areas you would like to see/experience growth over the next year.

_____

_____

_____

_____

- Make three declarations as to what you are willing to do for each item listed above. Please be specific.

_____

_____

_____

_____

_____

- What are the limitations/barriers to accomplish growth/ success in the areas listed above?

_____

_____

_____

_____

_____

- What does success in the areas above look like?

_____

_____

_____

_____

- How will you know you have accomplished your goals?

_____

_____

_____

_____

_____

- What support do you need from family to evidence the growth expected?

  _____

  _____

  _____

  _____

  _____

- Write your favorite quote or scripture as an anchor to remind you of your goals.

  _____

  _____

  _____

  _____

- Who are your accountability partner(s)? Please list their name(s) and ask them to support you on this journey.

  _____

  _____

  _____

  _____

  _____

Life Declaration I

Don't Overthink It

Before we dig into this section, I deem it necessary to understand the process of thinking from both the biological and practical perspectives. I will also take a few minutes to address cognition and metacognition. For those of you who enjoy biology and chemistry, this section should prove to be rather interesting. For those who don't, just keep reading. I am confident you will learn something. I am not going to unpack it thoroughly, but just enough to gain insight to better understand why we overthink things in the first place.

By definition, thinking is the action of using your mind to produce ideas, decisions, memories, and so forth. Thinking in itself is an operation of freedom. It is the human process of using knowledge and information to make plans, interpret and model the world, and constructively interact with and make predictions about the world in general. Psychologists have agreed that thinking is an intellectual exertion aimed at finding an answer to a question or the solution to a practical problem. In summation to clinical conversation, thinking is the action of utilizing processing skills to conduct cognitive activities such as problem solving, storing, and accessing memory, as well as to speak and interpret language.

As humans, we can think about what we want. We can dream and imagine what we want. We also can change the way we think once we purpose it in our minds to desire an alternate route in living and being. Thinking is automatic, which means it is an action that is without prompting. Brain activity is constant even during sleep. In fact, thinking and learning are cemented during times of rest and sleep, which is why it's critically important for children and adults to get adequate rest.

Thinking exists as the top mental activity demonstrated by humans. All human accomplishments and advancement come from the results of thought. Civilization, knowledge, science, and technology arise from the thinking process. Thought and activity are inseparable. Humans normally perceive an action in their minds before undertaking an activity. The brain's primary building element starts with brain cells known as neurons. Chemical processes in the brain send out messages through the neurons that determine the mental processes along with thinking. Granted, there is much more to this process. This is simply an introduction.

Cognition in Relation to Metacognition

It is often difficult to distinguish the difference between cognition and metacognition because they are closely related and often overlap. Developmental psychologist John Flavell described an example that I am paraphrasing. In essence, he stated that when people are reading a chapter from a book, they may ask questions to themselves about the information in an effort to improve their knowledge base. This is a cognitive function; it is an action used to improve one's learning or understanding of a concept. However, metacognition is the monitoring of the thinking. It is you questioning your questioning of the process in which you seek answers.

Cognition is a mental process that includes memory, attention, producing and understanding language, reasoning, learning, problem solving, and decision making. It is often referred to as information processing, applying knowledge, and changing preferences.

Metacognition is a subdivision of cognition or a type of cognition. Metacognition is defined as the scientific study of an individual's thoughts about his or her own thoughts. You are assessing your own thinking *through* thought. It is the way you think about how you think about things. That may be redundant, but I truly want you to understand what metacognition is. It will all make sense once we address the impetus of this chapter, which is to not overthink situations.

Brain-based Trauma

Okay, thank you for your patience. The science teachers are probably eating this up. Good; I am glad. Understanding how perfectly and wonderfully God made us is necessary in understanding why we should always turn to Him when we have questions about ourselves. And to that end, to the educators and parents, I trust you understand how important it is to stimulate the minds of your students and children each and every day. You must engage them in critical thinking and brain-based activities that lead to the production of new brain cells. The creation of new cells indicates the acquisition of knowledge or the processing of new information. When new brain cells are formed, this is a clear indication that students are learning and their minds are retaining new information.

We must continually challenge the thinking of children and young adults. We have to ask questions and create scenarios that force them to think critically, thereby challenging their cognition with alternatives that produce objective arguments based on evidence rather than subjective rants saturated with emotions.

This is also the case for faith-based leaders. The community you represent needs your voice and intellectual challenge to climb out of the hole life placed them in either by nature or nurture. There is no benefit in keeping people disenfranchised or oppressed due to race, economics, or mental health. You must have a mind-set of growth, innovation, and service. It is imperative that you actualize your calling to serve the least and the last as though they are the greatest and the first.

Our children are being exposed to violence, sex, drugs, prostitution, abuse, and a host of other societal ills that are stripping them of their innocence. As a result, we are raising a generation of unprepared thinkers who have a jaded, depraved sense of reality filled with hatred, bitterness, violence, and at the conclusion failure and death. Fragmented and broken, our children are filled with pain and agony. Our children and unrehabilitated adults see life through their experiences. They see life through their trauma. They see life through their pain.

This is where metacognition enters the equation.

Our youth may have a mind-set of change, but reality through the eyes of environment and nurture has shaped their thinking in such a manner where they mirror their mentality influenced by environment. As practitioners, advocates, and interventionists, we must show them a different reality, create a new paradigm, and show them a world where their existence matters and their futures are bright. Educators and leaders, this is the influence you have each and every day in your schools, classrooms, and churches. Regardless of the venue, we have to show them a reality full of hope, peace, and security. Once that is in place, learning is possible! Time is of the essence for our young people. They need your support in *reclaiming their time.* There is an enemy gunning for this generation. We can't afford to lose them without first putting up a fight. The fight is in the minds. Cultivate their minds in a way where critical thinking is the expectation. Do not accept their emotional disposition. Do not be turned off by their nonchalant, reluctant, and seemingly disrespectful attitude. Beyond the veil is a scared boy or girl screaming for help without the vocabulary to articulate it.

Now that you understand how the brain works, can you blame our children for being reluctant to learn and acting disengaged from achievement? In their cognitive function, they question what they have been through. They attempt to seek answers to uncover why there is so much pain, abuse, and isolation. They might ask, "Why is there no one in my life to love me, care for me, hold me, assure me, feed me, spend time with me, or at the very least protect me?" And because such questions are often unanswered, children begin to formulate their own answers. The danger in this is they do not have the experience or the wisdom to respond rationally to the questions they pose. They have postulated that they are not regarded or worth the effort, and as a result, they act out their frustration with rage. They perform it day in and day out until one day they end up dropouts, incarcerated, unsocialized or dead. They live out the reality that has been created for them through actions that resonate with their level of thinking about how they see the situation (metacognition).

Overthinking

I know that was heavy, but so are the issues. Our families are worth fighting for. School leaders and teachers, faith-based leaders and pastors, our families and our overall communities are counting on us to show them that they are worth fighting for and that their lives matter. Antwone Fisher posed the question, "Who will cry for the little boy?" One of us (or all of us) must respond with a resounding, "I will!"

If you recall, the title for this life declaration is "Don't Overthink It!" It is now time to wrap up all the brain-based psychology and trauma into a nice bow so that you can free yourself from the cycle of overthinking. By definition, overthinking means to think about something too much or for too long.

Some choices and decisions are not that difficult. If the decision is good for you, your family, or your faith, then do it. Don't overthink it. The thing that keeps us bound and shackled to our past is the critical analysis of events that have a degree of relativity to previous failure or disappointment. Because this scenario feels familiar or is associated with past disappointments or pain, we will talk ourselves right out of the action because of our thoughts and memories. And though I sympathize with you, overthinking will keep you in place of stagnation. It's a cycle of complacency and fear. Overthinking produces a drain on your time. Imagine how many hours you spend lamenting a situation. If we are going to ever truly *reclaim our time,* we must escape the trance of overthinking. And what happens is you don't even realize you are doing it; it is a trick of the enemy. Something that can change your reality for the better is trapped between mundane activities and passive thoughts about why you should not take a leap of faith. Shake yourself free from psychosis and aggressively seek an alternative that will transcend conventional thought. You deserve it. It's your time! *Give Me a Year!*

Because of what you have endured, you converse, argue, debate, convince, negotiate, promise, commit, rationalize, justify, and plead with yourself to do something that you do not have the courage to do. As a result, you waste a considerable amount of time. Retrospectively speaking, some hesitation and paralysis in thinking may not be your fault, but if you do not change the outcome based on your thoughts and memories, what is not your fault will become your problem. Your reluctance to break the cycle of overthinking will keep you at a level beneath your privilege. I don't know about you, but I refuse to live beneath my privilege. *Give Me a Year*!

Trauma in childhood that is not addressed or rehabilitated becomes a lifetime prison sentence of overthinking in adults. Can you imagine how long you have been agonizing over past hurts? I know it hurts. I know you did not ask for this, but it's with you—and it's up to you what you do with it. You are the variable. Either you can use your history to catapult you to the next level of your life, or you let it continue to be a drag hindering progress. If you do not foster and embrace a new reality through modalities of support and counseling at some point in your life, you will pay for it later. You can't bring a fixed, abused mentality into a reality of prosperity. It won't last, and that fact has been proven time and time again.

Psychologically speaking, it does not work. You will be trapped in a cycle of uncertainty and doubt, and as a result you will have wasted more time. I say no more of that. We are here to reclaim your time. We can't waste another unforgiving year overthinking every situation. Is he the one? Is she the one? Should I start a business? Can I really make a difference? Did God really call me? How do I know this is for me? If you are honest with yourself, how many of you are in this very place, asking the same or similar questions? Like Aibileen said in *The Help,* "Ain't you tired, Miss Hilly?" I now ask you a similar question: Ain't you tired of being broken and in a cycle of overthinking and overanalysis in every situation? When is enough going to be enough? You know God has given you a dream, a goal, and a vision, but because of either previous hurt or failure, you second guess a new reality each and every time God tries to offer it to you. This type of thinking is toxic and will stifle your growth. It will kill momentum and keep you at the level of "just making it." That is not the promise God has for me, and it is not for you either. Reclaim your time and put it to use for you and your family. Now is the time. Don't overthink it!

Personal Reflection

I used to overthink everything. What to wear, what to eat, what time to wake up, where to go to church, how much money to spend, whether God can use me, whether God is calling me, where to live, what job to take, whether I should write a book, whether I should buy this house, whether I deserved a family, whether I was equipped to lead, and on and on. I asked so many questions that I usually forgot what the issue was. It was a cycle of overthinking and second-guessing. I was trapped in the inner recesses of my mind. I have experienced some significant trauma in my life, and as a result, it stalled my growth and deactivated my confidence in making decisions. Man, I am trying to help somebody! I feel liberation as I type. Deliverance is in this section. Let's go deeper.

As an adult, I experienced the death of a sibling, extreme poverty while possessing two academic degrees, unemployment, underemployment, relational heartbreak, lack of sincerity in personal relationships, embarrassment and humiliation both professionally and personally, repossession of vehicles, and lack of utilities during the most inclement weather conditions (no heat in the winter and no electricity in the summer—and y'all, I'm from Houston, where it is unbearably hot in the summer). The feeling of inadequacy, no true sense of identity, and all this occurred after the age of twenty-one. I illuminate this point because there was no one to blame. I could not pin this on my parents. I was a full-fledged adult going through periods of suffering and maturation simultaneously because of decisions I made. I became resentful, bitter, and distrusting of not just people but also of myself.

Friends, what I had to realize was I was not cursed

though at times it felt like I was all alone. But that was not the case. I was being humbled and prepared. God had and still has magnanimous plans for me, but truth be told, life was wearing me out and it hurt. I endured lies, sabotage, and persecution and there was absolutely nothing I or anyone else could do about it. It was my season to be ripped. Did I embrace it in the beginning? Absolutely not. Did I think I was cursed? You better believe it. But today, I am thankful for the ripping. See family, ripping brings about change. It produces a harvest in what was a deserted place. And even Christ, who is the author and finisher of faith was brought to a place of discipline and obedience because of the things he suffered. Hebrews 5:8 says that even Jesus learned obedience by the things he suffered. Suffering brings about virtue, humility, honor, respect and purpose. In essence, I was ripped for a reason!

So after tumultuous rounds of suffering and judgement, I stopped being a victim and started standing as a victor. I made the declaration that I wanted my time and life back and was going to make effective use of it moving forward. See friends, money can buy you several things, but the one thing it can't buy you is time. Though I make statements about reclaiming my time, the impetus of the statement is to no longer waste time feeling sorry for myself or living very passively and then making excuses for a lack of execution, drive and determination. I am now going after everything purposed and desired in my heart.

I had to stop feeling sorry for myself. I had to grow up and realize that I wasn't cursed, that I wasn't undeserving of God's love. I was going through a season of preparation. God was preparing me for something greater. He was breaking me from all that arrogance and toxic thinking, and He was showing me that not by my might, but by His grace and power, do things change. As a result, I started unraveling the entanglement of unfruitful thinking and started breaking free from prisons to which I shackled myself. In many instances, I shackled myself to poverty and failure, but as I matured in my thinking and began trusting and believing in the love of a forgiving God and a dying savior, confidence in my decision making was restored. This is for you, Calvin: in his poem "If," Rudyard Kipling says, "If you can trust yourself when all men doubt you but make allowances for their doubting too." I started trusting myself again. I knew I was surrounded by skeptics, but I could no longer be one too. I had to believe in myself just as you have to believe in yourself. Get free from overthinking. Take this next year and commit your words, actions, and deeds toward breaking free from mental prisons erected by previous failures and unnecessary overthinking.

I've stopped overthinking as often as I used to (I am still a work in progress) and now trust that the architect of my life knows how He designed me and is able to provide technical support when it is necessary. God doesn't move when we want Him too. He moves when the time divinely coincides with opportunity. I am still putting the pieces of my life back together, but I am overthinking situations less, which is how I ended up in Ohio. I heard the call to do ministry in Ohio by way of leading a school. Because I love and respect my family, I asked Cornelia and Roman for their permission to travel to Ohio. Without hesitation they agreed, and here we are today. We're making a better life for ourselves, and as a result, we're making things better for a select group of people in Ohio. Not only that, but because I said yes to the call, there is now a Houston delegation in Ohio. Rhema, Calvin, and Carlton also said yes and are doing quite well for themselves. Rhema works in customer relations involving finances, Calvin is a professional educator with a calling on his life to lead schools, and Carlton is a model-based systems engineer. Three African American men with a total of four degrees between them are in Ohio and making a difference in a deserving community—all because they trusted and did not overthink the decision. They stepped out on faith and are better for it today. Many decisions aren't that difficult. You have to trust God in and out of season because at the end of the day, He is the one who adjusts the thermostat of our lives. Don't overthink it during this *Give Me a Year* movement! The reclamation of time is at hand.

The Declaration: Don't Overthink It!

You have to be audacious in your approach to break the cycle of overthinking. If that mind-set is not fixed, you must break it. It is God's desire that you be liberated from a spirit of cycles—cycles of failure, fear, anxiety in decision making, and stagnation. You may not know what to do, but like Nike says, "Just do it!" The *it* is something. **DO SOMETHING** to break the cycle and advance your life forward. You can't continue to overthink your life, your call, your profession or your ministry. To the educators: don't overthink the state assessments. Plan effectively, unpack (deconstruct) the standards, create your formative assessments, and teach to the appropriate level of depth and complexity. Teach like a champion. Like Rita Pierson said, "Every child needs a champion." And believe it or not, they may not all experience success the first time; that is why we reteach. But if a child fails on your watch, does that mean you need to change professions? Does it mean you need to return to corporate? No. It means some kids require a little more time and attention because of existing gaps. It simply means you have to dig deeper and be more patient and intentional with that student.

Some things are beyond you even though they are before you. You have to make up your mind to not run from them. Don't overthink the ability of your students either. Make them perform by setting a high expectation for excellence in everything both they and you do. Take ownership of the time you have with your students. Don't overthink your call to educate. We need most of you!

Teaching and leading a school is a calling too. However, just like in ministry, there are some wolves at the whiteboard preying on vulnerabilities and weaknesses adding to a students' perception of inadequacy and abandonment, rendering them hopeless and insecure. They need the advocate in you. Don't overthink that either. Kids should never be bullied by teachers and administrators. If you see this, it is your business. Step up and show kids they are worth fighting for. But as for you, you provide more than instruction. You provide safety, love, and support. You can't overthink your existence in the profession.

To spiritual leaders: start your ministry and deliver a message of faith, hope, and love. Guess what? Everyone won't receive you. Too bad for them. Your job was not to fill the house but rather fill and feel those in the house. What we see on TV is not everyone's reality. You may never fill a garage, but that does not mean your ministry is not effective. It is about the quality of your ministry, not the quantity. There are megachurches in operation not preaching salvation, the blood of Jesus, or deliverance. They may be large, but they're not effective. However, there are some storefronts that are running the devil into an alternate universe. They truly love God and embrace the sacrifice of His only begotten son, Jesus Cristo … Jesus, the Christ. (I spoke a little Español for my Latino brothers and sisters. Hola!). My point is simple: size is not a measure of effectiveness. As you reclaim time in your ministry, stop measuring it inaccurately. If your church loves God and His people, don't overthink it!

You can't quit just because it doesn't look like the image you have in your head. Satan keeps imaginations in our minds, and when our reality does not match our imagination, we see it as failure and begin the process of overthinking. We start counting up the money we wasted, the time we wasted, the people who hurt us, the bank that rejected us, the parents who cussed us, and the kids who disrespected us. From all that, we begin to overthink our purpose and calling. I declare that you must cast down those imaginations and understand that for every no you receive, all you need is one yes. Have an expectation of yes and keep your enthusiasm high.

You are built for this. Don't let your thoughts get in the way of the best days of your life. There is still time to turn it around. There is still time to believe in a better today. There is still time to trust that if you just step out on faith and not convince yourself that you are wrong, you could truly be the lender and not the borrower. But again, you must break the curse of overthinking. When you feel yourself thinking about a decision that you made and hear yourself arguing with yourself about something that you know will be liberating for you and your family, ask God for the strength and determination to let nothing get in your way, even if that means getting out of your own way. You have to condition (discipline) your mind to perform in a manner that is indicative of the call on your life and the success you deserve. Once that level of discipline is achieved, you won't be able to talk yourself out of something you have behaved yourself into. Discipline and execution will eradicate unfruitful overthinking and death by remorseful decision making. As shared in the beginning, you can't stop yourself from thinking, but you can definitely direct your thinking with positive affirmations and quality decision making.

Though we are professing *Give Me a Year*, please know that it will not be easy to make decisions and stick to them without deviation. There will be times where you feel yourself vacillating and overthinking even the smallest of decisions, but we don't have to solve it in one day. Remember, you are asking God for a year to work on it. It takes time to recover from a mentality-based in trauma. Your thinking will evolve and mature in time, but you must be purposeful and intentional.

I remember when I could not pass the teacher certification exam in Texas. I used to tell myself I was studying, knowing full well I wasn't. I blamed everyone for my failures except the true culprit. It was only after I started being honest and decisive in my decision making that after the seventh attempt (yes, I said seven; I am not afraid of y'all!), I passed not only the content exam but also the PPR and principal exam. Now I'm a licensed superintendent. Too God be the glory! When honesty and solid decision making becomes part of the equation, you can accomplish anything and everything. But hypothetically speaking, what if after the seventh failure, in my overthinking, I decided to forego the call to educate, lead, and inspire? You would not have this book, there would be no *Today's Prince … Tomorrow's King* (shameless plug to my first book that is for sale), and there would be no Dr. Hill encouraging you to preserve and live the most amazing 365 days of your life. That, ladies and gentlemen, is the danger of not getting healed from previous failures and allowing your mind to keep you in a place of captivity.

The virtue to soar, achieve, and overcome is in you. Stop letting fear and doubt enter your decision-making process. Take the next year and get free. Start small and evolve. *Give Me a Year* gives you free space to grow and develop. Don't let this window close in your face. Get your life back and bring your thoughts under subjection. Discipline your mind to perform in the face of uncertainty. God is with you and so am I. Habbakuk 2:2 reads: How can two walk together? They must agree. I am with you, your family is with you and if you truly feel you have no one to walk and talk with, God is with you and He agrees with you advancing your life and legacy forward. The time is now to go in confidence and in faith. Accelerate your life unapologetically and don't let fear steal your joy. Bring your thoughts under subjection and live on top of your failures and let them carry you into an amazing year. You can do it! Don't overthink it!

Don't Overthink It!

Please take time and give considerable thought to the questions listed below. Answer with your honest, most intimate reflections in an effort to setup the most amazing year(s) of your life. Remember, you deserve it!

• What decisions have you made to accomplish your goals for the next year? Be specific.

_____

_____

_____

_____

• What opportunities have you talked yourself out of recently?

_____

_____

_____

_____

- Do you trust yourself to make decisions under pressure? Please give an example.

_____

_____

_____

_____

_____

- Is your family counting on you to make decisions for the good of all?

_____

_____

_____

_____

_____

- List three things you can do to prevent overthinking/ over analysis when making simple or complex decisions.

_____

_____

_____

_____

_____

- How will the next year be better for you and your family based on your decision making?

_____

_____

_____

_____

_____

- What makes you second guess yourself?

_____

_____

_____

_____

- What steps will you take to override self-doubt?

_____

_____

_____

_____

_____

- Is your doubt/overthinking steeped in fear?

_____

_____

_____

_____

_____

Life Declaration II

Don't Live in Fear

Welcome back! I am certain many of you took a break after "Don't Overthink It!" It was pretty heavy, but that was by design. The goal of that chapter was to break cycles of encore (redundancy) that produce nothing. You have a golden opportunity to ask God for an unbelievable, mind-blowing year. *Give Me a Year* is about so much more than things. It is about you reclaiming and unlocking your righteous mind. It is about you running through barricades and obstacles and freeing yourself from prisons you were never supposed to be in. You deserve so much more.

Give Me a Year is a campaign of retribution to all who have existed in lack when abundance was next door. I am so thankful to God that he gave voice to this mission and has now converted it to text. But we have to walk in deliverance each day of our lives. If you think it is going to happen because you say it, you are sorely mistaken. This is a journey of faith. You have to exercise your faith. You have to walk it, talk it, profess it, claim it, invest in it, fight for it, rest in it, and celebrate because of it. Romans 1:17 states that the righteous—not the right now, but the righteous—shall live by faith. There has to be a continuation of sacrifice and commitment beyond the pages of this testament in order for it to carry you through the fulfillment of your days. But here is the good knows: all you have to do is take one step forward, and God will take two! *Give Me a Year!*

As is our pattern, let us define fear. Fear is an unpleasant emotion caused by the belief that someone or something is dangerous, is likely to cause pain, or is a threat. It is an emotion caused by anticipation or awareness of danger. Fear can make you anxious or concerned.

Fight-or-flight Response

We defined fear. We recognize and respect the fact that fear is a part of the human condition; it is fundamental. We have all experienced fear, concern, or anxiety in our lives, and that's okay. We understand that fear serves a purpose as well. Its purpose is to make us aware of a threat or attack. Again, we have no problem there. The issue is when fear is not a companion that visits when necessary. We are protesting the residential fear that keeps us sitting on the couch while the parade of growth and achievement is marching by our door. We can hear the music as the band plays ESPN. We can see the beads being thrown from the floats, we can smell the food, and we can touch the excitement (yes, I am talking about Mardi Gras), but because we had a bad experience or are not sure what to expect, or because people will look at us funny for enjoying ourselves, the parade passes us by year after year. That, my friend, is the fear we are exposing and hopefully evicting today.

The body produces chemicals and hormones that control our responses. Think about it: you know when you are angry, sad, or happy. You also recognize that for the most part, you don't have much control over that. That is because they are hormonal and neurological responses to a stimulus. Something foreign or from the outside is stimulating a response, which is causing chemicals and nerve cells to respond with involuntary responses.

Fight or flight is one of the chemical responses I am speaking of. By definition, fight or flight is the instinctive physiological response to a threatening situation that readies one to either resist forcibly or run away. The fight-or-flight response, also known as the acute stress response, refers to a physiological reaction that occurs in the presence of something that is mentally or physically terrifying. The response is triggered by the release of hormones. In response to acute stress, the body's sympathetic nervous system is activated due to the sudden release of hormones. The sympathetic nervous system stimulates the adrenal glands, triggering the release of epinephrine (adrenaline) and norepinephrine (noradrenaline). This results in an increase in heart rate, blood pressure, and breathing rate. After the threat is removed, it takes twenty to sixty minutes for the body to return to its pre-arousal levels.

And there you have it: the response to fear. Again, it is biological and chemical. Not much you can do about imminent threats of danger. But again, the fear we are speaking of keeps you in a position of wonder. "Dr. Hill, what do you mean when you say wonder?" When I say wonder, I am speaking of scenarios such as these: I wonder what would have happened if I'd said yes? I wonder what would've happened if I'd gone to the interview" I wonder where they are now? I wonder how much weight I would have lost by now? I wonder how much money I would have made if I had invested in the Snapchat IPO when it hit, knowing that I had the money to do it, but I let fear and uncertainty stop me from making millions of dollars with an investment of ten thousand ... Oh, sorry. That one was real. See? My fear cost me a multimillion-dollar investment.

Fear will bind you if you are not careful. If you remain in

fear too long, it will become part of your normal condition. It will infect your cells like cancer. In cancer, one cell becomes infected. After that, the proliferation of malignant cells begins to consume a region of your body. The only way to remove it is through an invasive procedure. Well today, that is what we are doing. We are removing the cancer of fear from our minds so that we can have a fearless rest of our lives, because each of us deserves it! *Give Me a Year*!

God Did Not Give Us Fear—Give It Back!

Second Timothy 1:7 states that God has not given us the spirit of fear but of power love and of a sound mind. Wait—if God did not give us the spirit of fear, then why do we keep it so close? As with everything we have shared up to this point, it is a choice. You are choosing to live in fear. You are choosing to let life pass you by because you fear the unknown. You can't control life, and so you might as well let it go. Each and every one of us has attempted to control either people or situations. The question I pose to you now is, How did that work out for you? You can't control your parents. You can't control your spouse. No matter how great a disciplinarian you are, once they are of age, you can't control your children. You can't control your boss. You can't control the weather. You can't control technology. You can't control any of it. The only thing you control is how you respond to it.

A good friend of mine is a financial planner. One of the most profound things I have heard in quite some time is the RNS concept. I was a bit confused because I was not privy as to what RNS represented. In short, he said, "It is not my job to push a person into investing. Neither is it my job to convince a person to invest. It is my job to recommend 'n suggest." Well, in the scenarios listed above, that is all you can do. When dealing with other people, all you can do is recommend and suggest. But at the end of the day, people are going to do what they want to do. Such is the case with you. You have the choice to engage in life any way you choose. The question is how confident are you in your abilities to get out and live without fearing failure and defeat?

Fear has robbed you of so many wonderful moments. I want you to really think about how fear and overthinking double-teamed you and prevented you from accomplishing, experimenting, or enjoying so many wonderful encounters life affords. Fear has an agenda that it takes great pride in executing. The agenda is to rob you of time and resources, to rob you of wealth, health, and prosperity. God did not give you a spirit of fear, so stop living in it. Fear is not your friend; it is a chemical response used to alert you of a threat. But for many of us, fear has overstayed its welcome. It has a front-row seat from the inside of your mind and emotions. It is time to break the lease with fear. Fear needs to be evicted—today. It has stolen so much time from your life, your profession, your marriage, and your finances. Evict it, eradicate it, expel it, and start reclaiming your time. It belongs to you. Fight for it! Remove the interloper. Ask yourself this question: When was the last time fear paid rent? If you think about it, fear has not profited you. In fact, fear has cost you time and opportunity. Put a stop to it today. Radiate the cancer and surgically remove any residue associated with fear. It is your great gettin' up morning. Don't live in fear for one more second!

The Declaration: Don't Live in Fear

Now that we've acknowledged fear is not our friend and should never be invited in for dinner or even a glass of water, what do we do to get rid of it? How do we live without fear keeping us paralyzed and in a position of lack? The antidote is simple: live with purpose, not fear. You don't need permission from me or anyone else to live with confidence. Confidence is welcomed; fear is not. You have all the rights and privileges to express yourself freely. What we can't afford is for you or someone you know to live in fear of rejection, disappointment, or regret. These things happen. I have been rejected more times than the law should allow, but guess what? It hasn't stopped me from asking the necessary questions, and neither has it prevented me from making an application. Rejection is a part of life. You can't be afraid of being told no. No is two letters that when they are reversed—uh oh, it's ON now! No is not as bad as it thinks it is, because once God says yes, *no* gets turned out to *on*. That's good news.

You can't be afraid of being rejected. You are not going to get every job you apply for, and neither will you always get the guy or girl you want. But guess what? You didn't need those things anyway. And while I am on a roll, stop giving people the ability to control your destiny. People are fickle and will always let you down. Educators, stop fearing what your principals think about you. They do not have the final say as to your outcome or existence. No one holds the patent on employment or promotion except for God! Last I checked, according to Deuteronomy 8:18, "for it is He that giveth thee power to obtain wealth." Yes, you respect those in power and submit to authority, but they do not define or own you. They do not control your destiny. When opportunity meets preparation, then you receive confirmation from God, through man, with an offer of employment, promotion, and in some cases termination. Termination is not always a bad thing when God is trying to transition you for a new thing. God gives increase, not man. People truly believe they have power over you because they sit in seats of authority. They Don't! It is God alone that has the final say.

Pastors, show your parishioners you can serve them. Spiritual leaders, embrace your community. Superintendents, love on your principals and teachers. It is not about you. Servant leadership is something in which you should take pleasure. Honor those who honor you. Place yourself in a position of support, not dominance.

I want us to be free of fear. My goal is to place you in a position of power and authority because that is the spirit God gave each of us. When people have positions of perceived authority and dominance, but then they don't use their position to coach and mentor you and rather demean and condescend you, then they are the ones with the problem, not you. Let me be clear: I am not telling you to be disobedient or disrespectful, but I am reminding you to not be a drop off for other peoples' shortcomings. Don't embrace or carry the insecurities of others as your own. You do not have the problem—they do. They are afraid of your abilities. They are fearful that you may expose their vulnerabilities and weaknesses. They are fearful that innovation will push them out of their roles. You should never apologize for being yourself. God gave you the spirit of power, love, and a sound mind! You are not crazy. Stop worrying; get off the gas. Do not be afraid of other people's insecurities. Never apologize for being confident. Live without apology or excuse. Work hard to reach your goals. Be confident in your abilities.

You don't need permission to be free. Unhook yourself from the bondage of fear. If you lose the job, you will get another. Or maybe God is trying to position you to start your own business. Only you and God know the answer. If you lose the relationship or the marriage, that's too bad for them. But that does not mean you should never love again. You can't be afraid of rejection or a repeat performance. You must learn from it and make adjustments for the next person. Also, don't live in sickness. You may have a disease where there is no cure. Don't be afraid of it—accept it, understand it, learn about it, and then fight it. You have to call sickness by its name and demand it leave your body. Study spiritual warfare, but beyond that, adjust your diet. Stop eating processed foods. Investigate a plant-based diet. Do something, but don't live in the shadow of death. The sun will shine again if you don't succumb to fear.

In the event that this is the end, enjoy your time. You are still here. Don't let fear keep you bound. I can't promise you it's going to get better, but I do recall in Isaiah 38 when Hezekiah did not want to die. He was not ready to go. He turned to the wall and prayed, and God granted him fifteen more years of life. If God did it before, He can do it again, but you can't be afraid to ask. But the answer will not always be yes. The Apostle Paul asked God in 2

Corinthians 12:8-10 to remove the thorn in his flesh. We are not certain what he was wrestling with or dealing with. It doesn't matter. What we know is that Paul asked God on three separate occasions to remove the issue. It was not until the third time that God responded and shared with his servant, "My Grace is sufficient for thee: for my strength is made perfect in weakness." It was at that moment where Paul realized that God knows I have an issue. I, therefore, need to take pleasure in my issues. There is nothing I can do about them. God's strength is made perfect in my issues. It is not because God can't heal all, it is more so important to God that you walk with Him long enough that the issues don't even matter anymore. Let God Be God even with your issues, sicknesses and diseases. You can't stop the inevitable, but defiantly don't have to be afraid of it!

Here comes a big one. If you lost a child, I know it hurts. It is a pain steeped with memories that produce great joy, but it is equally matched with immeasurable pain. You are afraid to live again, afraid to be happy again, and afraid that it may happen again with one of your other children. I understand, but you have to let those who died rest in peace, not in the sorrow of your pain. Scripture states that on the seventh day, God rested. Each of us will take up our rest at some point. Don't take the rest from your children because they have to be concerned about you from beyond. Please, let them be with the Lord so both you and them can be free. Please! Parents who have endured this, your pain and fear are costing you precious time to enjoy the good days God has predestined for you. You can't grieve or guilt God into doing anything for you. He gave you power and a sound mind; you have to use it. You can't be afraid to love again. You can't be afraid to connect again, and you have to embrace the reality that life is full of pain and misery, but that a life unchained from fear can be enjoyed and embraced.

To all, I close with this: please live the remainder of your days without fear. My son, when he was a baby, used to say, "It's not good for me?" I would respond, "No, son, it's not good for you." Fear is not good for you. Live free from that intruder. Evict him and replace him with confidence and joy. Enjoy the rest of your days without fear and overthinking. This is your opportunity to reclaim your time. Walk into your season. Don't live in fear! *Give Me a Year*!

Don't Live in Fear

Please take time and give considerable thought to the questions listed below. Answer with your honest, most intimate reflections in an effort to setup the most amazing year(s) of your life. Remember, you deserve it!

• What are you most afraid of?

_____

_____

_____

_____

_____

• What steps have you taken to overcome this?

_____

_____

_____

_____

_____

- How much time has fear stolen from you? Be specific.

_____

_____

_____

_____

_____

- Does your fear stop you from living?

_____

_____

_____

_____

_____

- List two things you want to try but have been too afraid to attempt.

_____

_____

_____

_____

_____

- Where would you like to see yourself in one year (personally, career, fitness, faith, etc.)?

  _____

  _____

  _____

  _____

  _____

- List three conscious steps you can take to not let fear keep you trapped from experiencing life.

  _____

  _____

  _____

  _____

  _____

Life Declaration III

Reject Reproach

Good morning! It is 3:06 a.m. on July 13, 2018. Since answering the call to compose this book, God has had complete access to my sleep schedule. I write when He tells me to write. I sleep when He allows me to sleep, all while working my job with diligence and honor. I am adding this for a reason. Obedience is not an option. Submitting to authority of any kind must be done with reverence and humility. We must be obedient when working in our calling. There is no place for laziness, arrogance or complacency, which are drains on progress.

We must be obedient when asking God to use us. I made a statement approximately two weeks ago to Pastor Lorenzo Brown in Monroe, Louisiana. I shared that I want

God to use me. My exact words to him were, "I have a yes in my spirit and my mouth. I simply don't know what I am supposed to be doing." Two weeks later, I am writing my second book: a gift for leaders and teachers who labor in the redemptive love of Christ. I am so thankful and humbled to be on this journey with you, but I must finish this assignment. This next life declaration, "Reject Reproach," will be graphic, but it is honest and necessary. It begins with the heinous atrocities associated with slavery. It is not for the faint, but it is written for all. It is with a spirit of humility and reverence to my ancestors that I write this next section. I love each of you, but we can't ignore the truth.

As I shared, I was awakened by God early this morning to complete this section. How many of you remember Alex Haley's *Roots*? It's the story of Kunta Kinte from the tribe of Jufuere, who was kidnapped and transported to these United States. Once here, Kunta was forced into American slavery. Because that is established, I can move forward. In my dream, Kunta was being bound and elevated to be exposed and shamed. He was about to be flogged. Please keep in mind this was the last thing I saw before being awakened. Not a good dream, to say the least. Mind you, I have not seen *Roots* in quite some time, and to be honest I was not in the mood to see him beaten. What I realized soon after I awakened was that the lashing I was about to view was not the message. If you recall the movie, Mr. Ames, the overseer, makes a statement. He forces the entire slave camp, including children, to view the flogging. He insisted that they all be present. Kunta—an African full of pride and courage, a Mandinka warrior—was someone to pattern after and give the other slaves hope. He was finally being elevated, finally being lifted, but not in the manner deserving of a man with his pedigree. He was being elevated to be scourged with one of the most primitive instruments to inflict pain. Kunta was being introduced to public shame and private reproach!

Unpacking Reproach

By definition, reproach means an expression of rebuke or disapproval; a cause or occasion of blame. It's an action to dishonor, discredit, disesteem, or disgrace. Reproach equates to shame. Shame is a painful emotion caused by consciousness of guilt, and it is a condition of humiliation and disgrace. Moving forward, I will interchange the two words to show relevance. Reproach is a mental prison associated with guilt, dishonor, and shame. The goal of reproach is to remind people of their embarrassment or fall from grace. It continually plagues their self-esteem and confidence. It maligns their drive and desire to accomplish their goals or dreams.

In this instance, and in the countless other times slaves endured such treatment, reproach and fear was the goal of the flogging. Kunta was severely whipped for attempting to escape. He was punished with an immeasurable amount of force. The trauma to his body was tremendous; the pain was inconceivable. But the reproach was irreparable. He was ripped for wanting to be free. He came from a land where he had family and friends, where he was regarded as a man. But he found himself in a place where he was shamed and abused as though he was a petulant child or a stubborn animal in which neither was the case.

The reproach endured at a public event such as flogging or lynching is something no man or woman should ever endure, but my ancestors and the ancestors of so many others did. Again, we are not rejecting the physical pain inflicted on the body—that goes without saying. But can you imagine the mental condition of the slave after enduring such a disesteeming event? Talk about trauma!

Reproach is a mental condition that can't be ignored. Think of the pain slaves endured mentally from being stolen or sold away from their family, friends, and country; stripped in every essence of the word (physically, emotionally, psychologically, culturally, linguistically); and robbed of their dignity, honor, and self-esteem. Then to add insult to the human condition, they endured abuse and torture at the pleasure of their cowardly, insecure oppressors.

The shame associated with these events pushed many to welcome death rather than subject themselves to the injustices predicated upon Africans. Shame and reproach are very real words with a tremendous impact on the psyche of the weakened—not the weak. Make no mistake about it: there was nothing weak about an African. In Africa, men were kings and women were queens. Africans were well trained (disciplined) and extremely strong both mentally and physically. But when they were stolen from their home country and shipped across the ocean, the trauma caused a condition of paralysis and fear. Again, I reiterate that there was nothing weak about an African. However, the residue from shame does not easily wash away. Reproach is a condition that, if left untreated, will keep your mind in shackles for the remainder of your days. Let's take this lesson to the children of Israel.

Exodus 1:8 reads, "Now there arose up a new king over Egypt, which knew not Joseph." Move down to verse 11, and it states, "Therefore, they did set over them taskmasters to afflict them with their burdens." There was a new pharaoh in power, and this pharaoh was not familiar with the contributions Joseph, an Israelite (Hebrew), had enacted through his gifting from God to save the Egyptians during a time of famine and desolation. Because of his obedience, humility and service, Joseph received great honor and prominence with the Egyptians.

The new king, who did not know Joseph, was insecure. He commented earlier in the text that the Israelis were too great in number and at any time may choose to subdue us and take us as their slaves. Because he lived in fear, but was in a position of power, he then placed taskmasters over them and thrust them into slavery. He also went as far as to have newborn babies killed, which is how we got Moses—but that is for another book.

Joseph served God and Egypt well. If you are not aware of the story, Joseph was sold into slavery by his brothers. Joseph went through a range of emotions. He was scared, angry, and depressed. He probably cried often as he reflected on the rejection and injustices predicated upon him by his brothers. I am certain he was afraid and very embarrassed about his demise. But Joseph never stopped believing. He trusted in God and committed his life to Him. He remained faithful, but more important, he embraced his situation. His bondage did not consume him—it promoted him. Though he was taken as a slave, he overcame the reproach (shame) associated with his bondage and trusted God for a day of deliverance. And when it came, he made the most of it. But once that covenant ended, shame gripped and blanketed an entire nation.

The children of Israel endured centuries of bondage and reproach by the hands of the Egyptians. As stated earlier, the story of Moses is for another book. In fact, I paint a very vivid picture as to Moses's contributions in my first book, *Today's Prince ... Tomorrow's King*. For those of you who have not read it, you should pick up a copy; it is a great read for men of color. Okay, back to the story. God sends Moses to deliver the children of Israel from their bondage but not their reproach. Because of what they had endured, they could not embrace a mind-set of freedom. They were overwhelmed with a new reality that was foreign to them. Freedom! They murmured and complained. They did not trust the deliverer (Moses) or the deity (God) who had organized the rescue mission. They had been in captivity for hundreds of years. They could not fathom the notion of being free. Fear robbed them of their inheritance!

Have you experienced this condition? You have endured so much in your life that you are not certain you deserve liberation? You feel enslaved to a life that is undesirable. Guilt and shame have consumed you. You have prayed and cried for a day of redemption, but that day never arrives. You are aching for a release, but you are not sure how to approach a life where there are no oppressors or taskmasters. You believe you are beyond repair, fragmented and broken and not deserving of repair. If that is you, please keep reading because this is your year to shed the layers of guilt, shame, and reproach that are keeping you bound in captivity. Emancipation is coming. Please be patient. You will not be a slave to anything or anyone ever again. *Give Me a Year*!

Personal Reflection

"We are overcome by the blood of the lamb and by the words of our testimony" (Revelation 12:11). This is why I share personal stories. It is my goal to help someone else overcome. Like I shared previously, you hold other people's salvation and liberation in your hands. They are looking to you for direction as you walk through the valley. They are observing how you address fear and transcend reproach. People need an example, someone who can model victory after a tumultuous defeat. That strength and resolve is coming to each of you. Get ready!

I was twenty-four years old. I prayed earlier in life to be a principal by the age of thirty-five. God heard my cry. Exactly ten years later, three weeks before my thirty-fifth birthday, God remembered me and answered my prayer. I was so excited. I was the new principal of Jack Yates High School in the heart of Third Ward, Texas. In Houston, we replace the name of the city with the name of the neighborhood. For instance, I bought my first house in Pearl Homes, Texas, and when I was a teacher, I taught in Sunnyside, Texas, at Sunnyside High, which is actually Evan E. Worthing High School. While I have a moment, shout-out to a true Southside living legend, Dr. Ronnie C. Evans Sr. He hired me first. He mentored me first. He embraced me as a son in this profession, first. Houston has its own distinct culture and traditions. I know they don't replace names where you are from, but in the land where it just don't stop, this is the way we ball! All my Houston people, did you see what just happened? "I chunk up the deuce from the south and the north. Boys talking down and boys wanna hate."

Okay, let me get serious again. But who knows? Next year, "I might buy Worthing!" Just a little regional fun. And let me add this plug too: smile more. Release some of that tension and anxiety. Smile and enjoy where you are. Smiling and laughing is very healthy. Do more of it as you break away from fear and shame.

I was so proud of this answered prayer. I was going to do amazing things at Third Ward High. I was going to be there for five years and introduce an educational system of honor, growth, and achievement. Students were going to emulate me, and my staff was going to embrace me. The community was going to love me, and central office was going to revere me. It was a beautiful dream, but it was so far from reality. None of what I depicted took place, except for the part about the students. The students were great. They had needs greater than I expected, but we grew up together. I introduced the statement "Do What's Right," which I'd adopted from my second educational mentor, Dr. Steve Fullen. The kids embraced the phrase and started curbing adverse behavior. The culture was changing. Kids started believing in right and wrong again. A moral code entered the building, which transformed the academic climate as well. My students were awesome, and I am proud of them. They grew academically, socially, and emotionally while I was there. We saw some impressive gains as they related to student progress and fiscal solvency, and we also increased the enrollment and graduation rate. It was a lot of hard work, but my team and I pulled it together.

But there is a very dark side to this story. I was not well received by a small delegation of the alumni association. They felt they knew better than I and my team as to school governance. I recall this statement made by an alumnus: "We don't need a suit wearer in charge of our school." I wore a suit every day. "We need someone to whom our students can relate."

I asked the alumnus what would be more appropriate. I asked, "Shall I dress like you?" This individual wore sweats, jerseys, and T-shirts all the time. He had no response. That was a depraved mindset.

Here is another example of what I endured. We embarked upon a 1:1 campaign in which each student would receive a laptop to engage in twenty-first-century learning opportunities. An alumnus who was against the program told me, "When I was a student, we didn't have laptops, and look how great we turned out." He then went on to insist that these kids didn't need laptops either.

I retorted with, "You went to school in the eighties. Laptops didn't exist." These are two examples as to the level of unevolved, underdeveloped thinking that I encountered on that assignment.

But please hear me out. I had some amazing supporters who recognized the work we were doing. They did not buy into the misguided thinking of the loudest people in the room. Many of the parents, alums, and community members rallied behind me and our cause. For those of you in leadership, you know as well as I do that it only takes a few to make the experience unbearable and intolerable.

Now to accelerate this story. I pray I am helping somebody with my honest reflections. There was a demonic force working against the school. I knew I was on assignment. I prayed over the grounds and hallways each and every day. I had some really good teachers in that building who cared about the kids. These teachers put their needs to the side and sacrificed day in and day out for the kids.

And then there were teachers who exploited the kids and negatively influenced them. I took a stance against wrong, and as a result, I paid the ultimate price. A campaign was waged against me. Their vehemence toward me became personal and malicious. I was lied to, conspired against, and accused of all manners of evil. I was a victim of home invasion. They spoke about me like I was less than a person. They staged a protest, conducted audits on financial transactions, and tried implicating me in a grade-fixing scandal. I was a victim of fake news and was written about often in their scandalous, salacious blogs. The list went on and on.

But in their infinite wisdom, what the cameras and disgruntled alumni did not catch were the students came to me each time they attacked me and asked what they could do to help. They were furious about the lies and the way they were attacking their champion. They truly loved and respected their principal. Leaders, always remember why you do what you do and for whom you do it. I had to show them how to walk through the valley of the shadow of death and fear no evil. I could not succumb to the shame and embarrassment, but the lies and attacks hurt. My kids saw me endure the shame, but my being focused on educating them was worth its weight in gold. They saw a man stand strong in the midst of adversity, and that is a testimony I will never take for granted. I modeled resilience.

I mentioned two events, a staged protest and a grade-fixing scandal. Let me now, after four years, break my silence. The alums convinced eight students to organize a protest based on the movie *Selma*. The adults, while exploiting children, wanted to protest school safety and gun violence. I'm not sure why gun violence was on the agenda. During my tenure, there were two guns found. Please notice I said found, not used. One after school and one during the instructional day. Both were dealt with swiftly without casualty or incidence. There was no issue with gun violence. Ninety plus percent of the staff, students and community were oblivious to the fact. The only ones impacted were the ones in the area.

To address school safety made very little sense as well because discipline had also improved. Suspensions were reduced, as well as fighting. But this is how desperate they were. They used YouTube videos of previous fights before my time in an effort to attach them to me. News flash: there are time and date stamps on the description.

Anyway, the great eight, as I call them, were to organize and recruit students to walk out the school at 9:00 a.m. on a Tuesday morning. It was about sixty-four degrees with not a cloud in the sky. The media was in place, and the teachers had been instructed by me to not obstruct the doors; if they wanted to exercise their right to protest, we were to allow them to do so. Around 8:30 a.m., the great eight were checked out of school by their parents. They did not walk out—they were checked out so they could be checked back in without consequence. Where is the courage in that?

The hour was approaching. We had a transition bell around 8:57 a.m. If the kids were going to walk out, this would be the moment. Ladies and gentlemen, not a single student walked out the building. They all went to class, and believe it or not, they were on time. Kids walked by me and said, "Mr. Hill, look at them out there," speaking of the great eight and their parents. "If they are so concerned about safety, why go outside where the guns are?" The school is the safest place."

I smiled and said, 'You're right, but they have a right to be there." On the inside, I was high-fiving them and saying the exact same thing. On the Jaden Smith version of *The Karate Kid,* Mr. Han tells Dre, "There is no such thing as a bad student, there are only bad teachers." The great eight were being led astray by irresponsible, immature, uneducated adults. But what I took pride in was the students who followed the teachings of their principal, who evidenced care for them each and every day. They remained in place and attempted to continue on with their education.

I will say it again: not one child walked out the building. It was now close to 9:15 a.m. The news cameras were packing up, and the great eight were checking back in with their parents. I was prepared to greet them with a smile because they were led astray by adults. Do you recall me stating earlier that there were some very evil adults in the building as well? Adults who had been possessed—I mean persuaded—to do harm to kids? One of those unscrupulous teachers was determined to give the people a show, and as a result, engaged [pulled] the fire alarm, which forced an evacuation. There was no protest; there was a false alarm predicated against my building at the hands of an imposter educator. That person may have had the license but not the morals, ethics, honor, or integrity that is supposed to accompany it. The images you see on the Internet are not of a protest but of a forced evacuation. And my students were not happy. And in the words of Forrest Gump, "That's all I have to say about that."

Second, I mentioned allegations centered around grade fixing. In a nutshell, in the state of Texas if you tamper with or alter grades, you will go to jail and lose your certifications. Here is how I respond to that accusation: I have never been to jail, and I have all my certificates. In fact, I just renewed both my teaching and principal license for another five years! There was no truth to any of it. Our students completed a robust, aligned academic unit to redeem time and credit. As a secondary attachment to academic work, our students also committed acts of service to the school for two reasons,

1. There is nothing wrong with providing community service to your school. It builds character and supports a culture of pride and excellence.

2. Most important, we logged the hours for students in the event the college of their choosing had a community service requirement. Everything we did was about positioning our students for success.

We were providing our students a service. Contrary to what you may have heard or believed, I was not forced out of Jack Yates High School. No one made me resign. I walked out on my own recognizance because I knew there had to be a better way to make a difference! I've heard all the talk, and I know there is a person who even takes credit for my perceived demise, but hear this: You didn't break me. Your antics elevated me to an international platform! So from my family to yours, thank you very much!

And again in the words of Forrest Gump, "That's all I have to say about that!" Man, that felt good. That last set was long overdue, a very cathartic moment for me.

Let me help you educators and leaders who have been through similar events: that type of release and testimony is a byproduct of prayer and forgiveness. Please know that forgiveness is not for the other person—it is for you. The more you forgive, the easier your transition will be. Like Christ, I have never spoken of these events. Even on interviews, I would not break my silence. It would upset Cornelia, but I knew my time to speak had not yet arrived. But because of this book, my time has arrived. I am liberated. Victory is mine! As Jekalyn Carr sings, "It's my winning season, and everything attached to me wins!" I am a blessed man with a blessed family. The secret is below.

> And the Lord turned the captivity of Job, when he prayed for his friends: also the Lord gave Job twice as much as he had before. (Job 42:10)

Here is the reason why I can firmly say I am over it. The shame no longer has a hold on me or my family. Reproach has had to release me and like Job … give me twice as much as I had before. Once I prayed for my enemies and friends, I was restored! *Give Me a Year*!

I took an extended amount of time to testify. Here is the reason why. I was on the news for things I did not do. I was flogged publicly and senselessly. All they did was wound an effective educator. Why? In an effort to shame me, to place me in a prison of reproach, to stoke and kindle fear and perpetuate a cycle of overthinking. And for the record, there is an added element of pain when you are innocent. These events, and events like them, were designed to destroy me professionally and paralyze me emotionally and psychologically. But I won't lie: reproach found a home in my mind. For the next fourteen months, I had very little confidence in myself. But God is faithful. I shared with you earlier that He will give you beauty for ashes. God has delivered me from Egypt and has provided me my manumission papers from the plantation of my mind. I am so thankful to God for his providence and provision. God is so powerful He performs international miracles!

Everything the enemy and his minions and imps did to shame me and my family has in turn blessed us tremendously. I want you to know that if your hands and heart are clear, keep fighting the good fight of faith. You can't live in the reproach or shame of other people's envy or insecurities. They can't help themselves; people attack you when they fear you. Always remember that. Unfortunately for them, I am not easily broken. I was trapped for a season. Reproach had consumed my mind and my body. It was as if I could still feel the wounds from my abuse when people mention Yates in conversation. It was a topic I did not want to discuss. I used to get called to job interviews just so people could hear what happened.

It was embarrassing and painful, and it was a level of public reproach I could not shake. But how many of you know that according to Psalms 37:23, "the steps of a good man are ordered by the Lord"? After reading that, you may ask yourself, "Well, what happened? What went wrong? This was the job you prayed for. Looks like it was a bad move." On the contrary. I just shared with you that my steps were (and still are) ordered by the Lord.

When we read that scripture, we have to include the bad steps too. We assume all steps have to be good, but that's not the case. God allows us to walk in some very dark places so He can be the one to turn the light of salvation on. All my steps are ordered. God is good to me and my family. I am a blessed man because of my trials. They tried to shame me and leave me for dead, but I declare that by His stripes, we are healed (Isaiah 53:5)! They laid stripes on my back, but because of the stripes on Jesus's, mine don't hurt anymore. Yes, the scars are still there. Google me if you don't believe me, but regardless as to what you read or think, "Ya boy is healed!" Now, run and tell that!

Give Me a Year!

The Declaration: Reject Reproach

I hope you are beginning to see it. I hope you are feeling the weights of bondage and reproach leaving you. We are asking God for a year to remove the stench of shame and reproach from us. I don't care what was done to you early in life or later as an adult. You do not have to own it any longer. The lasting effects can be cast down. Shake yourself free. Unshackle yourself from judgment, unconstructive criticism, scandal, reproach, shame, condemnation, low self-esteem, and failure. You are not a failure. You may have failed at something, but you are not a failure. Stop feeling sorry for yourself. Some of what you've endured was not your fault. Forgive your oppressors and move on. Remember, this is your year to be free. *Give Me a Year*!

Do you see the pieces coming together? You go through an attack, a period of desolation and despair, and you feel hopeless. You begin telling yourself how inadequate, ineffective, and worthless you are. You start overthinking the events and become immobilized. You can't move. You don't know what to do or where to turn, and so you do absolutely nothing except replay the events in your head over and over again. After that, you become fearful and distrustful of everything and everyone. You have a theory for this and a theory for that. You believe the world is mounting up against you. You are afraid to try, afraid to leave, afraid to explore. Fear has you bound and crippled, and here comes shame and reproach, ready to finish you off.

Not so. I declare that on this day, you will see the sun shine again. The clouds of overthinking, fear and reproach are repealed and replaced with confidence, courage, and honor. You deserve it.

Let us return to Kunta. He was strong and endured hardship and abuse. He represents every slave that was stripped of their pride, dignity, and self-esteem. They carried reproach with them at all times until either death or freedom. And what's funny is I am wearing a shirt commemorating Juneteenth. You may be a slave to one of the conditions we spoke of today, but I declare your liberation is here. Consider this book your emancipation proclamation rendering you free. You are no longer bound. No one can attack you any longer without your permission. They may carry a gun, but don't give them ammunition. Take back your life and live without shame and reproach. The dream of the slave is being realized in this book. An educated black man with a doctorate in education is writing about spiritual and physical freedom. My ancestors are rejoicing. Yours are too and are celebrating you. Give them a show!

You are not an accident. By now, you have to know that. In January 2018, I sent Cornelia to Ghana for twelve days because to be honest, Roman and I needed a break. I'm just playing, but she was there for a study abroad venture as she was finishing her master's degree. While there, she explored the western coast of Africa. She embraced new sunsets and horizons. She studied African history and ancestry. It was a very surreal experience for her.

I am referencing this trip for a reason. While there, Cornelia visited two very popular slave castles built by the Dutch. The castles were El Mina and Cape Coast. The castles were located on the Gold Coast of West Africa, which is now called Ghana. Though there were several, these two castles processed, branded, numbered, and boarded slaves until they were loaded in the belly of a ship to be *stolen* to America.

She stood at the door of no return. In the exact place where she stood, millions of slaves had endured that path of shame and degradation for what was an awful four-month journey through the middle passage. Once on the boat, those slaves never returned. They were not allowed to pack a bag or grab pictures to remember their loved ones. They left with pride, honor, critical thinking skills, and dominating strength and power. But she had an epiphany that day. Cornelia said, "For as many slaves who died and did not make it, my slave did." The slave who represented her lineage survived the journey and the institution of slavery.

I share the same sentiment with you. If you come from African ancestry, your slave made it. You are living proof of this. If they could endure their shame and pain, you can definitely rise above yours.

Let's go back to the children of Israel. They complained the entire time. Once released from their captivity, they continued to embrace a mind-set of bondage. The walk from Egypt to the Promised Land was no more than a ten-day journey, yet it took them forty years. Because of this, God allowed that generation to die out. Their fixed mind-set prevented them from entering into their well-deserved retirement village. In like manner, Moses received instructions that he would not be allowed into the land because of disobedience. Moses gave authority to Joshua. But here comes the good news. In Joshua 5:9, God told Joshua, "Today, I have rolled away the reproach of Egypt from you." For all they endured by the hand of the Egyptians, God removed the stigma of shame and reproach from His people.

Did you hear what I said? God is taking shame from His people. You have suffered long enough. You have to embrace a new way of thinking and living. Shame is no longer associated with you. You have an awesome opportunity over the next year to do some amazing things. Educators, find your passion to teach again. Leaders, find the energy to empower and encourage your followers again. Faith leaders and pastors, it's not over. You are not God, so you can't be perfect. Show your church a flawed man or woman, but rise above your shame.

It's not over for you either. We serve a forgiving God, a God of not only a second chance but another chance. This is your moment, your opportunity. Your steps are ordered; walk in them. The choice truly is yours, but I pray you take this day and get free from such toxic thinking. The past is in the past. Stop reaching backward. It's time to move forward. There is no reason to delay. Choose your life today! You are worth fighting for, and guess what? You deserve a season of victories!

Reject Reproach!

Please take time and give considerable thought to the questions listed below. Answer with your honest, most intimate reflections in an effort to setup the most amazing year(s) of your life. Remember, you deserve it!

- List two events that have caused you to live in reproach.

_____

_____

_____

_____

_____

- Have you healed from those events?

_____

_____

_____

_____

_____

- If you have, how? If you have not, what support do you need to overcome reproach?

  _____

  _____

  _____

  _____

  _____

- What steps will you take to free yourself from the bondage of shame?

  _____

  _____

  _____

  _____

  _____

- Have you forgiven the person or event that enacted the mentality of reproach?

  _____

  _____

  _____

  _____

  _____

- Do you believe you were intended to live a life of shame?

  _____

  _____

  _____

  _____

  _____

- In one year, what will you overcome that has caused you to live a life of shame? Please share how you will overcome it.

  _____

  _____

  _____

  _____

  _____

Until Next Time

I have enjoyed my time with you, and I appreciate your attention. Asking God for a year to get it right will be well worth it. It is the best thing you can do for yourself and family. *Give Me a Year* is for you.

Live without fear, be bold and dynamic, and most important, be honest and true. God loves you for who you are. He wants you to commit to removing sin from your life. He wants an authentic relationship with you. You don't have to live in the shame or mental paralysis of past failures and mistakes.

If you are willing, repeat after me. "Lord Jesus, I am a sinner. I have allowed sin to consume me. I no longer desire this lifestyle [be specific; call it by name]. Please deliver me from evil. I want to commit this next year toward _____ [be specific]. I need You in my life. I know You died for my sins and issues. I believe God raised You from the dead. I want to be saved. I invite You into my life. I belong to You. In Jesus's name, amen!

If you said that and meant it, it is my belief that you are now saved, for Romans 10:9 reads, "If thou would confess with thy mouth the Lord Jesus. And believe in thy heart God raised Him from the dead, thou shalt be saved." Find a church that teaches the Bible and speaks about the blood of Jesus. Commit the next year of your life, starting today, toward something that will truly bless you and break the chains that have been holding you hostage. The children of Israel were in bondage for 430 years. Break the generational curses attached to your name and lineage. It is now time to experience life more abundantly. This is your second, your minute, your hour, your day, your week, your month, and your year!

I leave you with this final scripture.

I reckon that the sufferings of this present time are not worthy to be compared with the glory which shall be revealed in us. (Romans 8:18)

May God continue to bless each of you. Until next time, **Give Me a Year!**

Reflections and Declarations

Use this page to position yourself for an amazing year and the rest of your life. Congratulations on making the choice to live the next year without overthinking it, without living in fear, and by rejecting reproach. Now, write your vision and let nothing get in your way!

Please write down the three goals you will accomplish over the next year.

_____

_____

_____

_____

How will you accomplish each of the goals listed above?

_____

_____

_____

_____

What are the barriers?

_____

_____

_____

_____

What fears do you have about the goals above?

_____

_____

_____

_____

How will you break the cycle of overthinking and uncertainty?

_____

_____

_____

_____

What does success look like for the goals listed above?

_____

_____

_____

_____

How will you hold yourself accountable?

_____

_____

_____

_____

What should you see in terms of progress in thirty days?

_____

_____

_____

_____

Sixty days?

_____

_____

_____

_____

One hundred twenty days?

_____

_____

_____

_____

About the Author

Dr. Donetrus Glenn Hill is a native of Saginaw, Michigan, but was raised in Shreveport, Louisiana. He is the son of Lillian and Donald. He has one younger sibling, Rondray. Donetrus shares life with the most phenomenal woman on the planet, Cornelia. Together, they share the joy of raising their amazing son, Roman. They have special children in Rhema, Calvin, Roget, Terrance, Kevin, and Carlton. Dr. Hill is a graduate of

Wiley College, where he completed his bachelors of science degree in biology and furthered his education by obtaining a masters of science in sports medicine from the United States Sports Academy and a doctorate in educational leadership and management from Capella University, where he was an honor graduate with distinction. His research design was centered on the cultivation of scholarly outcomes for at-risk and disenfranchised students.

Dr. Hill is a licensed minister that has delivered messages to various churches across the United States. Dr. Hill is a certified science teacher in the state of Texas, is a nationally certified principal in Texas and Ohio, and is a licensed superintendent in the state of Ohio. Dr. Hill is also nationally certified by the Center for Teacher Effectiveness to provide technical assistance in classroom management and differentiated instruction. Dr. Hill has conducted seminars and presentations to diverse crowds of educators both nationally and internationally.

Consultation Services

Dr. Donetrus G. Hill is the CEO of RJH & Associates, LLC., based in Houston, Texas. He is a senior consultant for Global School Consultants with national and international clientele for both public and private schools. Should you require technical support or professional services from Dr. Hill, please contact him using the following social media platforms.

LinkedIn: Donetrus Hill
Twitter: @DrDonetrus
Facebook: RJH & Associates, LLC.
E-mail: RJHassocites13@gmail.com
Website: www.donetrushill.com
Telephone: 281-217-9438

Dr. Hill is available for professional consulting, keynote speaking, and professional development presentations (half day or full day) in the following fields.

Scholarly Outcomes for Disenfranchised/At-Risk Students

Diversity and Equity Competency (Restorative Practices)

Leadership Team Development

Differentiated Instruction

Classroom Management

Student Engagement and Motivation

School Culture and Climate

If interested, please reach out to one of the platforms above. Don't waste another year not getting the technical assistance needed. Dr. Hill is available to support your organization in reaching its fullest potential.

Give Me a Year!

Printed in the United States
By Bookmasters